ROZE & BLUD

Miller Williams Poetry Series
EDITED BY BILLY COLLINS

ROZE & BLUD

A Poem by Jayson Iwen

The University of Arkansas Press
Fayetteville
2020

Manufactured in the United States of America

ISBN: 978-1-68226-132-3
eISBN: 978-1-61075-689-1

24 23 22 21 20 5 4 3 2 1

Designed by Liz Lester

∞ The paper used in this publication meets the minimum requirements of the American National Standard for Permanence of Paper for Printed Library Materials Z39.48-1984.

In memoriam

K. A. D.

1997–2016

CONTENTS

SERIES EDITOR'S PREFACE

When the University of Arkansas Press invited me to be the editor of its annual publication prize named in honor of Miller Williams—the longtime director of the press and its poetry program—I was quick to accept. Since 1988, when he published my first full-length book, *The Apple that Astonished Paris,* I have felt keenly indebted to Miller. Among the improvements to the world made by Miller before his death in January 2015 at the age of eighty-four was his dedication to finding a place for new poets on the literary stage. In 1990, this commitment became official when the first Arkansas Poetry Prize was awarded. Fittingly, upon his retirement, the prize was renamed the Miller Williams Poetry Prize.

When Miller first spotted my poetry, I was forty-six years old with only two chapbooks to my name. Not a pretty sight. Miller was the one who carried me across that critical line, where the "unpublished poets" impatiently wait, and who made me, in one stroke, a "published poet." Funny, you never hear "unpublished novelist." I suppose if you were a novelist who remained unpublished you would stop writing novels. Not the case with many poets, including me.

Miller Williams was more than my first editor. Over the years, he and I became friends, but even more importantly, before I knew him, I knew his poems. His straightforward, sometimes folksy, sometimes witty, and always trenchant poems were to me models of how poems might sound and how they could *go*. He was one of the poets who showed me that humor had a legitimate place in poetry—that a poem could be humorous without being silly or merely comical. He also showed me that a plainspoken poem did not have to be imaginatively plain or short on surprises. He was one of my literary fathers.

Miller occupied a solid position on the American literary map, though considering his extensive career and steady poetic output, it's surprising that his poems don't enjoy even more prominence. As his daughter became the well-known singer and recording artist that she is today, Miller came to be known as the father of Lucinda Williams. Miller and Lucinda even appeared on stage together several times, performing a father-daughter act of song and poetry. In 1997, Miller came to the nation's attention when Bill Clinton chose him to be the inaugural poet at his second inauguration. The poem he wrote for that day, "Of History and Hope," is a meditation on how "we have memorized America." In turning to the children of our country, he broadens a nursery rhyme question by asking "How does *our* garden grow?" Miller knew that occasional poems, especially for occasions of such importance, are notoriously difficult—some would say impossible—to write with success. But he rose to that occasion and produced a winner. His confident reading of the poem before the nation added cultural and emotional weight to the morning's ceremony and lifted Miller Williams to a new level of popularity and respect.

Miller was pleased by public recognition. What poet is immune? At home one evening, spotting a headline in a newspaper that read POET BURNS TO BE HONORED, Miller's wife Jordan remarked "They sure have your number." Of course, it was the day dedicated annually to honoring Robert Burns.

Miller's true legacy lies in his teaching and his career as a poet, which covered four decades. In that time, he produced over a dozen books of his own poetry and literary theory. His poetic voice tends to be soft-spoken but can be humorous or bitingly mordant. The poems sound like speech running to a meter. And they show a courteous, engaging awareness of the presence of a reader. Miller knew that the idea behind a good poem is to make the reader feel something, rather than to merely display the poet's emotional state, which has a habit of boiling down to one of the many forms of misery. Miller also possessed the authority of experience to produce poems that were just plain wise.

With Miller's sensibility in mind, I set out to judge the first year's contest. I was on the lookout for poems that resembled Miller's. But the more I read, the more I realized that applying such narrow criteria would be selling Miller short and not being fair to the entrants. It would make more sense to select manuscripts that Miller would enjoy reading for their own merits, not for their similarity to his own poems. That his tastes in poetry were broader than the territory of his own verse can be seen in the variety of the books he published. The list included poets as different from one another as John Ciardi and Jimmy Carter. Broadening my own field of judgment brought happy results, and I'm confident that Miller would enthusiastically approve of this year's selections, as well as those in previous years.

The poems in Jayson Iwen's *Roze & Blud,* winner of the 2020 Miller Williams Poetry Prize, are split into two sections, with a change of speakers in between. First Roze Mertha speaks, then William Blud. Iwen, the poet giving this pair the powers of speech, is a distant literary cousin of Robert Browning, for both poets are interested in how the human character—soul, really—reveals itself in speech. Get someone to talk long enough and the truth about them will be known.

Roze's poems enter without knocking. Here are few of her opening lines: "They shouldn't let men as young and beautiful / as Mr. Fiedler teach high school." "I love the smell of fabric softener on the breeze." "How can a boy as dumb as Ash Reed / make someone like me horny?" "I live with my real dad in a trailer park / on a ridge above town, / and Mom's already on her third husband, over in Wisconsin now." The subtle "town / now" rhyme in that last quote along with an ability to reflect on the bedrock themes of the beauty and the brevity of life hints at a poetic maturity that emerges as we wade deeper into her poems. Roze's downhome, earthy voice arises from her life in a "shitty little beautiful / trailer park." Her world, which smells of "Old Spice and cigarettes," is part of the familiar landscape of rural American poverty where the young die by drugs, car crashes, or their own hands. Iwen dodges the inherent dangers of sentimentality and anger by giving Roze a straightforward, authentic voice. She doesn't decry her disadvantaged life; she personifies it. A friend "dropped acid in the park / and woke up on Broadway." "Whenever neighbor Angie went on a bender, I knew / because her kids weren't at the bus stop in the morning." Through the natural cadence of her talk, Roze invites us into her life without making any more or less of it than it is.

Somewhere in this procession of poems, a shift occurs and Roze's language becomes almost unintentionally poetic. She "can hear the Berlin Wall falling" in the voice of a boy rocker. She can also hear "a church bell echoing / in the ruins of a city." As she becomes more reflective, the poems turn into existential meditations on the same obsessions that drove the poems of Keats or Yeats. Here's a sample: "We could go on into the unknown / and completely forget one another / until one distant day / we smell tomato soup and tuna / and think, Oh my god / that smells like something I ate / when I was in love." This group of linked poems leads to no conclusion other than Roze's maturation. Roze stares directly into some terrible truths (she calls pain "our final companion") but her final lines contain a limited hopefulness as she imagines the dead who will "die again in us / rise again in us."

William Blud, a former boxer and an aging Vietnam veteran, has graduated from the school of hard knocks. "I've known the intimacy of the world / mostly by blows, rib by broken rib / nose by broken nose." Shrapnel is buried "like treasure inside" him. An apparent victim of PTSD, he is haunted by memories not just of war but his childhood. "I awoke to the familiar sound / of artillery in the distance / but I lay on a soft bed. / Diaphanous blue drapes / rose and settled and rose again." He accepts the diagnosis: "It is a terrible condition, I know / but I am told it is only temporary, / that only the horizon endures." He is a man leaning against a lamppost in the rain, soaking wet; a man waiting for a friend under an overpass; a man who visits children's graves in a cemetery; a creature of winter; a kind of last-man-standing who is left to elegies about his dead friends and his dead wife, Mary. He has empathy for the animal world, a fondness for walking, and enough remaining grit and a bitter sense of irony to end his elegy for Mary with "I don't need to tell you / I always hated that cat. / There, I said it again." A vein of self-pity runs through these poems, but that is true to the aim of the dramatic monologue: to reveal character, no matter what. If the path of young Roze lies ahead of her, the path of William Blud lies behind him. Full of regret and sadness, he is best left with this alert apprehension in an empty parking lot "where a fox stands in the falling snow, / and nothing else moves / but the bouquets of breath / taken from us by the breeze. / The fox watches me, and I watch it. Neither of us will move / until one of us moves."

The poems in Judy Halebsky's *Sky of Wu,* finalist for the 2020 Miller Williams Poetry Prize, exist in a state of paradox, the speaker of this collection being poised between contemporary American culture and a China that is both geographically and chronologically remote. One foot is in the familiar world of bike rides to the movies and "T-back tankinis;" the other is planted in the simpler world evoked by Chinese poetry, which speaks in the primal language of "moon," "nest," and "wing beats." At several points, Halebsky seeks to bridge these two realms by writing letters to Li Bai, the seventeenth century poet known also as Li Po. The epistolary approach underscores the sharp contrasts between the two cultures. The results are sometimes humorous as the poet tries to explain the oddness of American life: "They sell beer in cans . . . I know, it's amazing."

At other points Li Bai, who "wants to meet Robert Hass," and his fellow haiku master Du Fu are teleported (why not?) into their future / our present, where they smoke cigarettes, ask about Charles Wright (not the one who sings "Express Yourself"), and play cards with a deck that's missing an ace. All this chronological play produces some jarring moments as when Li Bai orders a bourbon in a karaoke bar. Such moments come off as playful skits, but as a whole, this book is guided by serious intent. The environment is not ignored. Whales are disappearing. The globe's waters are rising.

Halebsky's stylistic range is on full display when she switches from pure observation (moon, water) to a kind of revved up American rap. This is how she likes her free verse: "I want it big like a cherry Slurpee, a boob job in an anime film, the biceps of a trainer at Gold's Gym. Bursting, pushing on prose, veering toward some movie script with popcorn and hair-salon updos and all the hours until dawn." In lesser words, she likes the unleashed energy of poetry, and in the poems gathered here, she delivers.

There seems to be no such thing as a typical poem by Angie Mazakis, whose collection *I Was Waiting to See What You Would Do First* is also a finalist for the 2020 Miller Williams Poetry Prize, mostly because this book is bursting with variations in form and sensibility. But here is a clue:

> The newspaper says,
> "Woman in Iceland
> Unknowingly Joins
> Search for Herself."
> She heard her own
> description and it was
> a resemblance she
> couldn't imagine, long
> eraser strokes softening
> her temples, eyes drawn too
> wide. She said "No one ever
> *discovers me,"* and even when
> she blew her *cover*
>   she was missed.

On display here are an attraction to oddities and a fondness for paradoxes, especially ones that collapse on top of each other. What follows those lines is "When I look / at a missing girl's / child photo, I don't know her, / but I feel like only / I know the nuances in her / face." Many of these poems present a provisional narrative which, by the end of the poem, is overwhelmed with asides. Mazakis tirelessly shuttles back and forth between the mind and the world, the psyche and the bus stop, creating a perfect mix of clarity and mystery. She seems to be as fascinated by the external world as she is by her internal life. Her most arresting insights occur when she allows herself to be distracted, or better still, when she becomes the distraction, then vanishes with it under her arm. The attention demanded from the reader by these poems is exhilarating.

Shifting planes of reality and intention make up much of the imaginative play here. In a poem titled "I Miss the Friday Train and Have to Take the Monday Train," we accept the suspension or disappearance of the weekend, but other entities slide in and out of focus as well. "Once I unexpectedly saw a person I loved in my hometown, and then my hometown was no longer my hometown, just a place he was and then wasn't anymore." Another poem is presented like a movie, that is, scene by scene, but here the scenes repeat or contradict one another, and characters walk "out of the frame" and reappear as extras. Turn the page and a love affair is mixed together with the predicament of a couple stuck on Everest, running out of oxygen. There's a poem consisting only of quotes from the TV show *Hoarders*. A favorite of mine titled "Aircraft Safety Information Pamphlet," begins,

> The cartoon guy lifting the raft has one hand
> resting on his knee like this is old hat, this
> releasing the raft from the aircraft.
> He's been here before.

Such helpful titles and formal patterning give the reader just enough reality to hang on to as Mazakis takes us on a freedom ride of associations, droll reflections, and strange observations. We know where we are going, then we don't. We are quickly moved from expectation to surprise and back again. And to entice you, here are a few of many local delights "We've agreed not to appear in each other's dreams" and "I make a face like I see someone I know outside the train, but they can't see in." Finally, in a poem titled "Illusions of Self-Motion," lies this lovely speculation on the consequences of gravity increasing in strength: "You pull gravity in close, / the stars compressing until Orion's cloak falls to earth." There are no apparent limits to the imaginative reach of Angie Mazakis.

Congratulations to all three of these poets. The press is honored to be the home for these titles for years to come.

Billy Collins

ACKNOWLEDGMENTS

I am particularly grateful to the following for reading earlier drafts of *Roze & Blud*: Joshua Bernstein, Martyann Birman, Julia Burhans, Chris Fink, Julie Gard, Kat Mandeville, and Bryan Tomasovich. I would also like to thank the following for their friendship and support throughout the endeavor: Kamal Abu-husayn, Francesca Abbate, Mark Bayer, Anthony Bukoski, Joe Cadotte, Xuan Chen, Flore Chevaillier, Rula Diab, Kathy Fagan, Huda Fakhreddine, Chad Faries, Deborah Faul, Elizabeth Grbavcich, Laura Jacobs, John McCormick, Heather McGrew, Elaine Meszaros, Ephraim Nikoi, Kate Nolin-Smith, Yvonne Rutford, Deborah Schlacks, David Tromblay, Ryan Vine, Adeline Viranian, Jamie White-Farnham, Sandra Woerle, Kyoko Yoshida, Scott Zieher, my big, boisterous family, and, of course, Billy Collins and the staff at University of Arkansas Press. Finally, I hope I have hereby honored my many teachers and students, my mentors James Liddy and Denise Sweet, and the citizens of the Twin Ports."Sunrise" originally appeared in the anthology *Home*.

"Evening" originally appeared in *The Freshwater Review*. *Roze & Blud* has also been a finalist for The National Poetry Series and The Green Rose Prize.

ROZE MERTHA

Sunrise

I live with my real dad in a trailer park
on a ridge above town,
and Mom's already on her third husband
over in Wisconsin now.
I had a big brother for a while,
from Mom's first marriage Out West,
but he went to Iraq and only half of him came back.
Sometimes I feel like I'm the other half,
haunting his old life,
but that's usually nights when Dad's on the road,
and I'm alone, and to make the feeling go away,
I curl up with Tiger on the couch
and we watch war movies in the dark,
and I smoke Dad's cigarettes.
Mom was drunk at the funeral,
moaning and crying things like
My baby is dead! and *I love him more than anyone else!*
and *Why did God do this to me?*
She left early to get more drunk
and everyone was relieved to see her go.
I don't hate her. I know that *Out West*
was some kind of Eden for her,
and she burned it down in grand style,
and she thought she could get away from it,
but it's burning inside her still,
and she drinks to put it out,

but that only feeds the fire.
I suppose you could say she's in hell.
And I'm just across the river.
Sometimes I sit outside on the steps
and imagine Travis sitting beside me.
"You shouldn't be smoking," he says.
"You shouldn't be dead," I say.
"Everyone dies," he says. "It's natural as the sunrise."
"What does it feel like?"
"Like coming home from far away."

After Praxiteles

They shouldn't let men as young and beautiful
as Mr. Fiedler teach high school.
When he stands beside slides of sculptures
and lectures on the progress of art,
he assumes the attitude of the bodies beside him.
And what we can see of him outside his clothes,
his face and hands, his neck and wrists,
are smooth and white as marble.
I follow the lines of him as far down his collar
and as far up his sleeves as I can,
and I want to keep going with my own hands,
following the flesh of him wherever it leads,
as if I'd just finished making him myself.
And then he pauses and looks me in the eyes
and says, "Roze, what is your question?"
And I go blank as a statue's eyeball
and shake my head,
and he says, "I know you have a question."
And I want to say so many things,
but what I say is, "What would you call it
if you made something like that today?"
And Mr. Fiedler smiles at me
like we've met in the middle of a wasteland,
and he says, "Well, I suppose one
might call it *After Praxiteles*."
Oh, Mr. Fiedler, beautiful, bright, and opalescent
Mr. Fiedler, who could ever say
you never had your say?

Fabric Softener

I love the smell of fabric softener on the breeze.
Friday evenings, when I'm done with homework
and waiting for Kat to come get me,
I sit at the picnic table that is our front yard
and try to forget everything that's ever happened to me,
the good, the bad, the everything between.
To be who I'm meant to be,
I don't need to take anything more than this feeling
with me into the future;
like Dad, now making his way back across the states,
I need to erase great distances
from the fabric of time and space,
from the great cosmic mess of memory.
The scent of fabric softener washes over me.
Someone else is removing the excess of life
from their clothes and sheets.
Someone else in this shitty little beautiful
trailer park knows forgetting is
the surest way to love.

Ash

How can a boy as dumb as Ash Reed
make someone like me horny?
Isn't there supposed to be something like evolution,
or a god, or gods, or at least something
as comforting as fate?
When we have to circumnavigate the track
in P. E., I walk the periphery,
and an irrepressible thrill of pleasure fills me
whenever his ass sails past,
and I curse myself for being more base than he.
And when it's all over, and they're lying
like giant cats, panting in the grass,
he smiles up at me and says, "Better late than never,"
and I smile stupidly, and I want to jam a pencil in my head,
and I want to choke him . . .
and lick him and ride him all the way to Cloquet. . . .
Then Kat pokes me in the ribs.
There's a rowan tree across the street from my trailer.
It's heavy with red clusters of berries
that nothing seems to eat but robins in the morning.
They choke them down,
as if there were nothing to savor but the need,
and I pray, to what I don't know,
that I am something more than a robin,
in the morning of a life,
famished by a long night's sleep.

Everyday Apocalypse

for the kids I babysit

Here's how I like to imagine
the beginning of the end:
two children are watching TV
when the TV shuts off.
"Turn it back on!" shouts the younger one.
"I didn't do anything," says the older one.
They inspect the set and the remote,
both of which are completely dead.
"Mom!" shouts the younger.
"The lights don't work either," says the older,
"and the phone's dead too."
"Where's Mom?"
"I think she went outside.
Did she say something before she left?"
"I don't remember. Did she go to the store?"
"I don't know. Let's look outside."
They climb the basement stairs
and go to the front door and unlock it
and step outside,
and the sky is bright orange,
and the street is empty and glowing and silent.
"Mom!" the younger one yells,
and they hear it echo.
A burning tire rolls over the top of the hill

and slowly down the street.
The children watch it.
Then the older says to the younger,
"Let's get our backpacks
and our adventure gear,
and let's find Mom!"
And that's how it begins.

What Good Parents Say

You can go anywhere
and do anything,
as long as you don't hurt anyone,
or hurt the Earth
(and remember that no good American
would ever leave for good).
The world is round,
so you can't fall off.
In fact, you can't escape.
So save the environment.
Save the animals.
Save us all.
Save yourselves.
Run as far away as you possibly can,
but stay in touch.
We love you.

Football Sabbath

Kat's mom tends bar weeknights
and tells fortunes Saturdays
in a head shop downtown.
Beyond palms and star charts,
she believes you can read the future in sports,
because, she says, a game's unwritten until it's done,
assuming Vegas hasn't rigged it.
It's pure fate unfolding before you.
She smokes a lot of pot
and told me once I'd live long
and be miserable most of the time.
She says she's a doctor of numerology,
astrology, and man-ology.
For example, if the Packers play the Vikings
when the Moon is in the fourth house,
and Peterson runs the ball
for more than one hundred yards,
ten days are added to the life of mankind.
Kat's eyes are the strongest eyes I know,
from all the rolling they do,
and Sundays are a blue haze
of incense and smoke and football
and cheese puffs and ice cream and pizza
and the future revealing itself to us
one yard at a time.

The River

Time again to shudder and convulse
and release another unborn soul
into its afterlife on Earth.
I sit silently bleeding in World History,
and I think of the armies sleeping inside me,
the millions of eggs in my ovaries
that came to be before "I" even did,
buried in my body like terracotta warriors,
to serve whom, for what purpose,
in what unimaginable future. . . .
Mr. Belker drones on,
and I hope I look like I'm taking notes,
but I'm thinking of them,
encamped on either side of me,
waiting for the next river of blood to flow
so they can leap in and be carried
away from this life of captivity.
Uh oh, Mr. Belker's looking at me.
Back to World History.

Starlings

Whenever neighbor Angie went on a bender, I knew
because her kids weren't at the bus stop in the morning.
After school I brought them sandwiches
so they'd have something other than cereal to eat,
and I'd sit and watch reruns with them
until she reappeared . . .
until they all disappeared last year.

When I was ten, and Mom and Dad and Travis and I
lived together in a real house, one day
Mom heard scratching in the water heater flue.
Dad ignored it for days,
until he couldn't take it anymore and unscrewed
the duct, and a starling burst out
and flew into the utility sink,
where it started drinking the soapy water
spewing from the washing machine.
Dad shook his head and grabbed it
and put it in a cage for me,
and I cared for it until Mom let him go.

I dream about them sometimes,
Angie's kids and the bird,
and each time I find them in a dream
they've been waiting for me,
as if their lives continue in my mind
when I'm awake, or away in other dreams,

and when I dream them again they ask me for food,
because I've been away so long,
they've been so long without it,
and I wake with a knot in my gut
and stare at the ceiling
and wonder how full my mind will be one day,
of dream beings waiting for me,
hungry and wanting to know where I've been
and why I can't stay.

Where Poetry Comes From

Last summer I joined my dad
on one of his cross-country trucking routes.
I'd never been further away than Minneapolis,
so I tried not to sleep, so I could see
how the country changed as we went,
the first day from woods to prairie to steppe
to a truck stop somewhere in Wyoming
where we ate dinner and then went back to the truck
and crawled into sleeping bags
in the back of the cab and said goodnight,
and, as I listened to my dad snore,
I thought about my mother growing up
in that half-alien, wind-blasted land
that made her so different than me.

When I woke, dad was gone,
and the truck was moving.
I leapt out of bed into the cab
where he sat in bright sunlight behind the wheel,
and I yelled, "Why didn't you wake me up?!"
"You looked like you needed the sleep."
"You know I wanted to see everything!"
"Sorry. I'll pull over for a bit

if you want to get a closer look."
"What good'll that do?"

Without a word he pulled onto the shoulder
and got out, so I did too.
Where we were I couldn't say.
I knew the names of nothing,
the land formations, the rocks, the plants.
I couldn't say anything about anything but us,
the truck, the dirt, the sky . . . and home.
My language was all back there.
All I could do was look around me
and say, "It looks like. . . ."

Lingering

And dad says it's time to get going,
and I climb back into the cab,
and he helps by giving my butt a shove,
but his hand seems to linger there longer
than it should, when I'm already up.
And when we're back on the road,
I sit beside him in silence,
wondering what the lingering meant
or if I imagined the lingering
and if I'm the one actually lingering
there longer than I should,
suggesting something I'd rather not,
but now, no matter how you slice it,
something is lingering between us
in the small space we will inhabit
for another three days,
in the small space we will inhabit
for the rest of our lives . . .
until one of us is gone
and the other one waits
for the space to return.

Ancient Technology

I love making Michael Hutchence
sing his satanic love songs to me
from the afterlife of a plastic disc.
I can hear the Berlin Wall falling
in his voice.
I can hear the nearly human yearning
of wolves at the edge of firelight,
the eerie sound of angel's wings
dragging across the ground,
needles in grooves,
needles in veins,
needles underfoot in hidden glades,
the scrape of blades across hide,
the clang of iron against stone,
voices from other lives
begging to take this one
past the edge of the last.

Tuna & Tomato Soup

True love isn't fate.
True love isn't eternal.
It is I could leave you tomorrow.
I could leave you tonight.
We could go on into the unknown
and completely forget one another
until one distant day
we smell tomato soup and tuna
and think, Oh my god,
that smells like something I ate
once when I was in love . . .
and I did nothing to keep it together.
And your whole body seems
to gather in your face
and want to get out.

Tina's Hair

Everyone's saying Tina Hanson died yesterday.
She got dressed up, skipped school,
got her hair cut and donated it to Locks of Love,
then went home and overdosed on her stepmother's sleep meds.
Tina: out.
Tina's parents: planning Tina's funeral.
Tina's brother: beginning a life of even deeper introversion.
The kid that got Tina's hair: dead of leukemia within the year.
Tina's hair: in a box in generations of closets,
until a stranger takes it out one day,
wonders why anyone would make such a small wig,
and throws it out.
Then to the landfill that seagulls circle in great, insatiable halos,
where Tina's hair is buried deeper than any grave.

Rain

When it rains,
it doesn't rain straight down,
but hits the windows
and walls all over town.

It soaks the shoes
of the former alcoholics
smoking under the awning
of the Tranquility Club.

Shadows huddled under
the park shelters
cackle and curse
and lean their heads closer.

The distant refinery flame
sags under the rain,
flickers, seems to die,
then rises even higher.

Night rises over day.
Rain falls beside us,
and on the good people
trying to sleep
under the 35/53 interchange.

Horns in the Harbor

What baby waking
to the terrors of its crib,
what gut-shot beast
bleeding beside the creek,
what old man lying sleepless
in a rented attic room,
reassessing his life too late,
who hears this very night
what I hear moaning over the water,
each tuned to the same source,
like echoes lighting up the hillside,
when blood reaches the end of us
and turns again toward the heart?

Keepers

I died two years ago,
and nobody noticed.
Teachers keep calling my name,
as if I'm there.
Kat keeps coming around.
Dad keeps making the brunch
I liked the most,
eggs over easy and ketchup on rice.

I was once happy just watching the sun set.
Now I'm one of the many dead
doing homework and clocking in
and stocking shelves at work
and studying the mirror
for evidence of the crime.
And I keep following the path
my body was taking before it happened,
moving forward, they say.

The Love of Influence

There are times, when writing,
my books spread around my bed,
I pause and hear the voice of another
echoing through my words,
and I feel a hand
has reached across an unspeakable divide
and settled on my shoulder
and gently rests there
as my pen returns to the page,
and I know, even in greatest despair,
I am not alone.

The Passionate Geek to the Jock

Come, Ash, to my estate,
the fourth trailer on the right,
and we will see what we can do
to help you pass Math 2.

Take off your coat, your shoes, your socks. . . .
(Is it too soon to doff socks?)
Take off whatever you
feel remotely inspired to,

and sit beside me on the sofa.
Would you like a can of soda,
or maybe beer? A little whiskey
can help with trigonometry.

Maybe later? Certainly.
Now, aromatherapy.
Do you prefer patchouli or weed?
No, I didn't say *weed*.

Relax, we're all alone. My dad
is crossing some desert in Nevada,
and my mother doesn't visit much.
It's just you and I and a couch,

and one way or another,
the two of us will discover
how to solve the conundrum
of two variables by making them one.

Beauty

If you wear the right pants,
the boys' mouths lower
like little draw bridges,
and out pours a blinding light
that fills the calendars
at abortion clinics
all across the state.
No matter how threadbare
your underwear—
they tear through it
like wrapping paper
Christmas morning,
children unwittingly
unwrapping the bodies
of other children.
And when that gift is revealed
we hate them for it,
and they go off and sulk
their own dark way,
and we put our perfect pants
back on, and they go back
to their terrible smiles,
and somehow enough of us survive
that someone manages
to make it all sound beautiful . . .
someone makes the pain possible
by taking it away.

Rings

I hate the way we talk about age,
beginning at birth and ticking off the days,
as if they meant the same to everyone.
Let me ask who's older:
a grandfather who's going to live
another twenty years
or a baby who's going to die tomorrow?
I say we assign age by how close we are to death,
not how far we are from birth.
The baby's ancient,
and tomorrow it's eternal.
Grandpa's younger than me.
I say we never ask and never know,
until the tree is down
and we can count the rings.

Beauty II

Rain falls from a cloudless sky
on the west side of town,
on the low income housing units,
the mountains of gravel
and logs waiting beside the tracks,
on the stubble of abandoned lots,
ditches littered with diapers
and beer cans and unraveled condoms
and here, in a pool of iridescent mucus
under the stop sign at Central and Waseca,
a thick tangle of earthworms
writhing in an ecstasy so profound
my heart breaks that I'm not a worm.
Then my heart breaks that I am,
and I walk on,
into a stranger rain.

Bonfire

1.

Tonight I wait for her
by the tree line behind the trailer park,
where they found the buried body of the boy
who owed his dealer too much
and went missing for a year.
That was ten years ago already,
just a fuzzy memory at the edge
of my childhood,
a vague dread emanating from the field
behind my home.
He was my age now when he went away,
and that feels like something,
so I come here sometimes
when I know someone is coming soon
to collect me,
and I talk to whatever's there:
"I saw pictures of you.
You looked beautiful and gentle and strong,
and I bet the world had better plans for you
than this," I whisper, "But I'm glad you're here.
Your life is like a precious stone inside my own,
a glittering I can see through the trees."
Then I'm aware of an engine idling by the road.
And there's Kat, behind the wheel,
blowing smoke out her window,
and I turn and whisper, "Sorry, gotta go."

2.

First we find the cars,
park a hundred yards beyond them,
then take a hit from Kat's pipe
and plunge into the night.
We know where they are by the beats
in the trees and the castaway lights
flickering through
to oblivious saviors.
Down the gravel path and into the black,
wading through brush
and smacked by branches
until the inferno rises before us,
the silhouettes of friends and lovers
and intimate enemies
passing like Plato before us.
These are the gods of the woods,
the gods of ravens and fire
and drums and beer and young men
and denim and regrets,
the gods of forgiveness and despair
and Old Spice and cigarettes.

3.

Techno throbs from the unseen,
and fire spits its teeth at the stars,
and restless shadows shuffle
from keg to fire to conifer and back.
Dezzy surfaces on murmurs
like oil on a stream.

Kat brings me a cup of beer,
and we sit in the grass at the edge of the light
and watch the silhouettes circle
(Chip and Dildo and BT
and Hoss and Teabag and Dori
and Scratch and Sniff and Franny)
until we spy the true center of their gravity.
Squatting on a log nearest the fire
sits Ash, taking long drags on a joint,
staring into the blaze.
He blows a deep blue plume
and flicks the roach into the flames.
Slowly surveying the circle, he says,
"She's never coming back.
I know it as sure as I know
this is my first life as a human."
His eyes settle on mine.
"You feel it too, don't you?
Like you've just been caught
and put in a zoo."

4.

The Dezzy speculation erupts:
Her stepdad grabbed her ass
and she ran away to LA
so her mom wouldn't go crazy.
She got knocked up by a Canadian
dealer who smuggled her
back to his farm outside Thunder Bay.
She dropped acid in the park

across from the bus station
and woke up on Broadway.
It goes on and on like this,
longer than anyone could believe,
until her ex-boyfriend Dave
stumbles into the firelight
protesting, "No, no, you don't understand,"
and falls over a log,
face down in the dirt, and lies still.
Then, on one shaky arm, tilts up
and falls flat again
and lies still.
Then, on two arms, rises
and turns and sits and watches the fire,
as if that were the plan all along.
You can usually know a man
by how he gets back up.

5.

The liquid wind washes over us,
and above, the clouds spiral away
from a moon lucid with indifference.
Night falls. The temperature falls,
and someone scoops Dave up under the arms,
and someone yells, "Let's swim!"
And strong arms are around our shoulders,
urging us up
and down to a ledge over the old rock quarry,
and they strip down to skin
tightening in the moonlight

flashing across their flashing forms,
muscles shuddering under the flesh,
nipples budding, about to burst.
And Kat naked beside me,
chanting, "C'mon Roze, c'mon!"
And I'm shaking my head,
saying, "Not tonight. It's too cold."
"Suit yourself, pervert!" She laughs
and leaps into delirious screams.
And here where I am, the liquid night,
the pines soaking up our human sound,
the first snow of the year coming down,
like conception,
out of great silence, dark and clear,
onto human ground.

6.

A sudden gust of snow rolls
out of the treetops and spirals out
over the edge of the pit,
and there, on the path along the edge,
a darkness thickens in the night,
into a figure that stands and leans
like someone familiar,
and, before I can think,
I'm whispering, "Dezzy?
Is that you?"
And it just stands, and I slowly approach.
"Dezzy, where are you? Everyone's worried."
The figure shifts, as if raising an arm

toward me, and I reach out and step
into a shadow cast by the moon
and a fir.
There's only darkness here,
unveiled by a clearing in the clouds
and the cries of those swimming
in the pit below,
as obvious, I suppose,
as any great revelation.

7.

Red and blue lights appear in the night,
flashing through foliage from the road,
and time turns into motion.
Kat is instantly beside me,
clambering into her clothes,
and up we go, through the trees
to the road beyond the lights.
Behind us are police cars and the figures
of our friends in headlight silhouette.
Ahead is our car, and we're in it,
crawling forward in the dark,
till we arrive at the first crossroad and turn
and turn on the lights and accelerate
away into time again,
Kat beside me, laughing,
turning the heat on full blast
and laughing.
I smile and mutter *I love you*
under the noise.

And her laughter keeps rising like a wave,
and I know one day Kat will leave us too,
that ten years later, when I'm working nightshift
at the gas station at the edge of town,
she'll come in for coffee and cigarettes
and she won't recognize me,
and I'll feel too ashamed to say hi.
Is that *love*?
Is that *life*?
Is that just the night and pine trees and moonlight
and the first snow of the season
and the cold, wet, ecstatic bodies
of beautiful humans speaking?
And I know we should never end with questions,
so yes, yes, and yes again.

The Weather in Green Bay

The center births the ball
and the quarterback cradles it
to his chest, steps back,
the line bending and groaning around him,
and tries to divine the future.

The temperature is dropping.
Everything is turning to ice,
the breath on our lips,
the sweat on our fingertips,
the blood on the grass.

Everything is getting slippery now.
The quarterback holds tighter
and soon too will we.
Even the earth holding us up
threatens to spin out from underneath
when we take off.

We are strong and we are nimble
and we are running for our lives.
All we pray for is a break,
to find ourselves open and free,
to turn and see the ball coming our way.

When that day comes
we'll clutch the slippery message to our hearts,
we'll dig in our cleats
and take it to the future.

But first we must be open.
We must be ready to receive.
We must run and swerve and not fall down
and warm ourselves with our own heat.

Out of the darkness above,
a snow begins to fall
into the light and din of the stadium,
into the camera's collective vision.

We can still see the ball,
rising behind his head,
though the snow is falling thick now
all over America.

Tiger

Tiger sitting in the window
watching the world fill with snow,
to what use do you assign
this vision in your mind?

Is it what you do not see,
branches lined with chickadees
and chipmunks gleaning beneath the feeder,
that swells your heart with memories of murder,

piercing cries, pungent smells
and tasty brains in crunchy skulls,
crickets, flies, and centipedes
popping between your gnashing teeth?

What do you see when you look at me,
an angel bearing cans of meat
or the biggest meal of all,
if you should outlast my fall?

What does it say about me
that my love should have such teeth
and I forgive such cruelty
to see you idle in the light.

Tiger sitting in the window
watching the world fill with snow,
to what use do you assign
this vision in your mind?

Boots & Snow

My feet are finally big enough
to fill Travis' snowboard boots,
if I wear two pair of wool socks,
so Kat and I hit the Spirit Mountain slopes
until our legs are too sore to go anymore
and we sit at the top of Super Pipe
and watch the lights of the city rise
and the snow fall from the falling dark.
And I know it's only night,
and this is only snow,
and these are only boots on my feet,
and we're only alive long enough
to know
only is all that matters.

Music at Dawn

When the snowblower stops
the subtle world returns
like clues to a mystery.
Pigeons coo under someone's eaves,
and a broken windchime tries.
Natural gas hisses through pipes
like distant harness bells.
Closer, the snow brushes
my bedroom window.
My heart beats so hard
I can hear it below the snow
and feel the blood moving in waves
through my toes.
I try to stop breathing but I can't.
My lungs shudder under a pain
that grows in weight
until the air tears my mouth open
and leaps inside.
Something, it seems,
other than me
wants me to breathe
and wants me to feel it.

Fetal

The last time I had the flu,
curled up in bed, under a pile of blankets,
shivering in and out of dreams, I looked up
at the shaft of dusty light pouring in
and heard the muffled voices of archeologists
and the scraping of their tools
and realized they were trying to find me,
to release me from the past,
and I tried to sit up, to call out to them,
but the pain was so great I curled up tighter
in the position so many of us take
in our final moments,
when we wrap ourselves around the pain
that is our final companion,
and we stiffen
into a human approximation
of the stone from which they deliver us one day.

Talk

for Kat

Let's crawl into the cave
of the human mouth
and make a fire there
to warm us by.

I've been outside the circle so long
I've forgotten the song
my mother's throat once made,
how it differed
from the cold, dark humming
between the stars.

Those moments the words
burn between us,
the wick of my tongue
catches fire, and the flame creeps down
to its glistening root
and ignites a light in my chest.

Let our talk awaken within us
the dormant seed of our start.
Let us bloom into the darkness beyond us,
from the cave
where we first set out.

My Dream

I am the ashen rain falling,
running in oily rivulets down tarps into rusty cans.
I am the dust drifting up to the eaves,
grey eyes glistening in the midday dark.
I am the sludge-thick bay struggling after the moon.
I am the blind, etiolated beast fanning its transparent fins
at the bottom of the sea, in a valley between freighters.
I am the white cricket roasting in the pan.
The homely glow of a car battery lamp
holding a ring of feral dogs at bay.
I am the frost on a baby's eyes the morning after the massacre.
The rats living on rat flesh in rat cages in the rat man's shack.
I am the flesh of the mythic fruit buried miles beneath a mountain
on an island in an arctic archipelago.
I am the dull disc of sun sunk in the boiling murk of sky.
I am the charred remains of the last astronaut stewing in a hubcap.
I am the one who will eat the men who ate her lover.
I will hang them by their Achilles tendons
and drain the blood from their throats
and burn it so the smoke rises
into the night where no eyes can see
but the eyes of indifferent gods watching over me.
I will turn their flesh into the flesh growing in my belly.
I will turn them to the future.
I am the snow that settles on the dead.
I am the photograph of a family taped

to the inner wall of an overturned dumpster.
I am a tooth broken off in a bone.
A bone broken off in a wound.
A wound broken off in a life.
A broken bit of glass casting a broken bit of rainbow.
I am a light casting the body of me.
I am teeth gleaming in the moonlight
deep in a northern forest,
running, running, forever running.
I am the Earth turning beneath my feet,
the sun rising into song,
the vast blackness beyond.

The Great Beast

There's a great beast within us,
with teeth the shape of our dreams.
It's large and dark as the universe,
but its eyes glitter just behind our own.
It peers into our lives
and sees what we will see when we sleep.

The beast has a black hole for an umbilicus,
rising up to its source
before space and time.
The beast is every tense but the present.
It taught us to hunt
and turn the intentionless earth to tools.

The beast is before me now,
leading me through the labyrinth of this poem.
A great flank slides by,
and a pain like the anticipated death of a child
pricks my heart.

Only when we are dead will the beast sleep,
faithfully curled around our memory,
until it is awakened by another race
and its cry is heard once more,
like a church bell echoing
in the ruins of a city.

Vessels

Though the ships are frozen in ice,
the winter sun warms our faces
when we smoke down by the docks.
In winter we come to see what isn't there.
In summer we come to watch the boats come in
from all ends of the Earth,
only to return in a day or two,
and we dream of where the sailors go,
like all our little creeks pouring into the sea.
At night we come to smoke beneath the Milky Way
where stars condense like rain drops
from evening clouds.
And we wonder out loud
where love comes from
and how you can wear your heart on your sleeve
when both are always changing,
and sometimes I wonder if I exist
only so these experiences can be,
if they can only live
through the shape of me.

The Way Back

I know where I'm going
is where I began,
but where was that?

An embryo
or an egg or sperm
or part of the bodies
of my mother and father
or the meals that made them
or the fields where the meals were born
or the sun and soil and rain
or primordial landscapes
of elements from the explosions
of primeval stars?

Or this very moment
where I have always been,
always am,
am always going to be,
as independent of the world now
as when I was an egg,
or a blade of grass,
or a star appearing in the twilight above
two lovers lying in the grass
of an alien world?

The Earth's Metabolism

Mayfly burns a life in a day,
cricket in a summer,
man a few more.
The weather washes over us
like waves over a shore,
green rising and falling
at the mercy of the light,
for millennia and more.
We are the Earth's
many selves
rushing forward into life
as our wavelengths incline,
one decision at a time.

The Dead

Every second of every day
the dead rise
in coils of root and smoke.

Every second of every day
the dead enter us
by eye, nose, and throat.

They live again in us,
die again in us,
rise again in us.

WILLIAM BLUD

Afterlife

Life was one explosion after another,
until it blew me apart.
And yet, here I am.

Sometimes men die.
And sometimes men die,
and then they live.

Rising

In the war we were soft beds
where bullets went to sleep
and sometimes dreamed
a life for us
back on the streets of our home towns.

And all about us burned the world.
The jungle was green flame
rising from the earth
and raining down on us again.
The children's faces, the sky itself, aflame
with time and expectation.

A slow fire burns
about me still,
eating away at the streets
and the once-familiar faces
and the memories themselves.

I draw my own hand
from the darkness beside me
and see it by a light
that rises through wires
from an ancient sea.

The hand too is a flame
rising endlessly from the earth
where the bullets still dream.

Touch

I've known the intimacy of the world
mostly by blows, rib by broken rib,
nose by broken nose. Over time,
it crushed one ear, slashed the other,
smashed a knee cap, snapped an arm,
shattered both orbital cavities.
It's slapped me, burned me, ripped me, stabbed me,
buried shrapnel like treasure inside me.

I have not wanted it this way.
I have yearned to rest this flesh
against something other than blows.
I have yearned even for a love without touch,
and the yearning burned in my gut
like a memory of illicit acts,
until, lifting a glass or tightening a screw
or gripping a doorknob,
I was aware I held what countless others had
and in that felt their hands.

Palpitations on a Park Bench

I used to know what robins sounded like
before a storm.
I used to know what it smelled like
just before the rain.

And when the rain came,
the confirmation
filled me with an ecstasy
that some small part of the Mystery
had been revealed to me.

I think there was something else
I used to know,
something supposed to remind me
of what it was I forgot. . . .

Where has it all gone?
Buried by deck maintenance protocol?
By the white squall off Fair Isle?
The New York Stock Exchange?
Vietnam?
The last hundred gallons of vodka?
The first?

There's something wet on my face.
What is this?
It has no color, no scent, no taste.
Wait, wait,
it's coming back to me now.

My heart feels
like it's about
to blow a hole in my chest.

Mother & Father

My first memory is of standing in the basement
of my first home in Superior,
watching Mother unpack boxes
with words written on them
that I was just beginning to understand:
bedroom, wedding, work. . . .
In my first memory, I know
Mother is making the world
a place to live in.

A light burns in the attic window.
Father has built his workbench there.
Sometimes I venture up the stairs
to watch his body lean
into a fine cloud of wood dust,
like a lover over his work,
turning life into furniture.

Though I am old now,
the light still burns in the attic,
and there are boxes yet to be unpacked
in the basement,
and all the work is left to me,
as it is to each of us,
to be both Father and Mother
to what remains between.

Dawn

The nearly black blue and sharp
cry of a crow cuts the cold
eternity of night, and light
of the same star that gave us life,
that some distant day
will reclaim it,
crawls over the horizon, slow and thick
and endless as an imperfection in a fingernail.
A familiar hand appears,
one that steadied you as a child,
and offers you the gun it used
to end its own life.
Ignore your unsettling dreams and sleep
now, or forever await
the return of a vision lost in the sun,
a pop-fly falling forever from on high.
Raise your own hands toward it,
and close your eyes,
and awaken.

Tijuana

All I can dredge from the wreck of that year
is a row of tequila shots on a plywood bar
and a long, moist donkey cock
glistening in stage light.
There's always more than we can remember
and more than we can ever know.

The performer leading the donkey home
through sun-bleached streets,
through the scent of baking tortilla,
to the tiny walled yard
where she strips again
and, squatting in a concrete basin,
pours rose water over herself.

The soapy bucket in sunshine
where the sad-eyed donkey stands patiently
while the children wash him,
their little fingers working the suds into his hide,
big brother describing the towers their father
is building into the sky over America,
a breeze blowing off the ocean,
ruffling the leaves of the avocado tree,
stiffening her flesh into pimples.
Mother drifting off in a towel,

thinking of her husband
balanced on a girder over a growling city.

Little sister raises her hand above her head,
and a bubble blooms between her fingers
and floats over the basin
and up past the curtains shivering in the window
where mother has already fallen asleep.

Oh, sun setting now on the ocean,
oh, Abuela sitting in the doorway,
oh, cool, dark stable in the corner of the yard,
oh, Father so far away.
Oh, to be with you now.

Horizon

My father visited me yesterday
in the shape of my son.
My dog Comet haunts the park
at the end of a stranger's leash.

I know for now these things
are not true.
I know they are the past
coming back for me.
And I know someday soon
they will be all I know.

The buoy is breaking free of its chain.
The land is everywhere
the sea once was.
The sea is everywhere
the land once was.

Mother and Father talking
endlessly back and forth across the table.
She turns to me now and frowns.
"Where has your father gone?"
she demands.

And though I see him everywhere
and am overwhelmed with love,
I am too afraid to speak.

It is a terrible condition, I know,
but I am told it is only temporary,
that only the horizon endures.

Who Knows

In my prizefighting years
I broke over fifty noses.
Where, I wonder,
are they now?

Nuzzling the air
inside pint glasses?
Regally saluting the earth
over their heads,
under stones
no one's read more than once?

Do they still float
like mine
toward suggestions of heaven
that turn out to be
backyard barbeques?

Do they still remember my right hand,
this thing already anticipating
its next life
as some kind of animal claw?

It loved them once,
this ugly thing.
It loved to make them new.

Brains

for Mark and Eric

The guy who dresses my deer
tells me every animal's got enough brains
to tan its own hide.

What considerate creatures we are,
to know enough to be
and be each other's cover.

I wonder, my sons,
when my memories of you are rubbed in,
will you make me shine?

Will you recognize me
from a lineup of any old skins
hanging in any old hallway?

Will you know me
from the clouds or the trees or the snow on the river,
when I was just one

of many convolutions
the world was making of your own brains
before I left?

When it was already awakening
in my own hide,
my own epitaph.

Good Death

for the deer

I hope to die as I believe you died,
walking out on an early morning ridge,
old battles aching beneath my hide,
to see the world fill with light, as if
revealed for the first time to the eyes of life,
and hear a crack of vast ice expanding
and unseen sparrows burst into flight,
from the center of me feel the world rushing
outward into the vacuum of all we know,
a flock of sparrows circling empty air,
a life setting itself down in the snow,
and hands descending to raise again to air,
to open, appraise, and lovingly convey,
to become one with the one who writes my elegy.

Passage

I was beaten already
by the time I boarded my first ship,
at the westernmost tip of Lake Superior,
deep in the heart of the continent.

The war had spit me out,
and I woke, still drunk,
on my mother's back porch,
and I walked two blocks to the lake,
signed the papers,
and climbed aboard an ore freighter.

As I painted the deck
I watched the continent slide by,
cliffs and trees and then cities,
a steady breeze at our back.
When we passed through the locks,
children at the railings cried out
and waved hello-goodbyes.

And then, one day,
the ocean opened up before us,
and there was no earth but us.
Nothing but the blue of the water

and the blue of heaven
and the blue of us hovering between.

And so we passed from the world
to beyond it
in one fluid motion,
from the terrible grip of life
into something as much like death
as anyone can know in this world
and yet bend to work
and yet rise to see
the blue eternity,
and breathe and know
somewhere back there still is home.
And between is nothing
but more of where we are.

Our Bodies

1.

They ship what they can
of our bodies back.
And what they can't
remains in the sand.

What we leave behind we someday inherit,
children standing beside our beds,
imploring us
in inscrutable tongues.

2.

I awoke to the familiar sound
of artillery in the distance,
but I lay on a soft bed.
Diaphanous blue drapes
rose and settled and rose again
in an inconstant breeze,
entering by an open window overhead.
I felt as if I were lying
beneath an immense blue
body of water,
the boom of Neptune's stride
approaching from afar.

A thin woman with bright black hair
floated into the room

and lay down beside me
and ran her fingers through my hair,
and I remembered her name was Rima
and we'd met in a bar somewhere in Jounieh
after the Captain had said we'd be fools,
but we could go ashore for eight hours,
and I remembered
I had better start moving
toward the sea.

3.

It's autumn now.
Frost is on the vine,
orange by every door.
People who once had little ones
are preparing for Halloween.

They bedeck their homes with death,
to draw the children near enough
to peer into their eyes
and see, for a night,
what they left behind.

We

The beauty of the street is threefold.
The street that is now,
cracked asphalt beneath a sea of mist,
and the street that was
sixty years ago, when I fell from my bike
and the memory became part of me.

Follow the street out of town
to where it becomes a country road,
then a gravel path,
then a pasture where we dismount
and walk until we stand beneath a towering elm
in the middle of a field,
and, as we look up at it,
it seems to look down at us,
and a chill creeps over us,
and then a rain.

And so
the beauty of the street is three.
We are what remembers,
and we are what is remembered,
and we are, all three of us, We.

Night Walk

for Jessica

1.

After they took you out of her
and she'd fallen into drug-induced sleep,
holding my hand,
I left Mary in her room
and went out for my first night walk.

I've just returned from my most recent
about ten minutes ago,
and not much has changed
between the two
but Mary is gone now
and I am an old man.

The night hawks still cry
over empty streets.
The humans have gone indoors
to bathe in the sterile blue
dreams of their screens,
and I walk through the darkness
of the world that is.

And I would like to say
you've missed nothing,
but to say so
would be to deny

that you'd ever been
and that you too are part of all this,
an old man walking the streets
of a world before dawn.

2.

That night, when I stepped out
of the hospital and stood
in the rain, I felt as though I'd just emerged
from a vast labyrinth of caves
where, until that moment,
I'd lived my whole life
by the light of torches,
and now I stood in an opening so immense
I felt myself expanding outward in all directions
and, in feeling no resistance to the expansion,
fell forward and steadied myself
against a street lamp.
I closed my eyes and pressed my forehead
to the cool metal of the lamp post
and felt the rain pressing through my shirt,
and I breathed deeply
and, holding the post yet,
looked up through the rain
and clouds and past the moon

and past the stars,
and the darkness seemed to grow in density,
until it was as solid as the wall of a cave,
and, I am sorry,
I took great comfort in that,
my little one,
great comfort.

Thread

Any moment a family could end.
We follow it, as we would a thread through a maze,
not knowing who left it there,
or if we are nearing an exit
or yet another entrance
or perhaps some place within the maze itself
someone once decided to make a home.

Merzad leaves his door open day and night.
He lies on a cot in the corner of his room,
propped up by pillows so his head rests against the wall.
About him hangs a perpetual haze of cigarette smoke,
illuminated by pale blue light
cast from an old television
he found at the Goodwill on South Tower.

I know his pain will not diminish with time,
but grow, year by year, as his children would have.
A strange thread has led him here
to a sublet in the center of a dream, of a nation,
with only a reticent old man for company.
I would make him wings of newspaper and tape if I could,
but we know what good that would do.

I can do nothing but set aside
the pain of my own failings and betrayals,
so I may keep pace with his sorrow.
It is the thread now that I follow
toward the only hope of a future we have,
here, in the next room.

Merzad's Sigh

Lighter than air,
yet the heaviest sound
I've ever heard.

A string running from his birth
to this moment,
before he lights another cigarette,

begins to vibrate
somewhere so deep inside him
known dimensions wouldn't allow.

Yet out it sounds
as seemingly slow and thick and leisurely
as an atomic plume

rising effortlessly
toward heaven,
and all those living

or soon to be
living
there.

Mary's Pussy

Mary's pussy enchanted me
when first I brushed against it
fifty years ago.
A bolt of unknown voltage
leapt into me,
and, how shall I say,
my heart leapt up.

Mary's pussy took me by the hand
and led me to Mary,
to the many Marys Mary became,
the bold Mary coming
to my basement door,
patient Mary waiting by the docks,
playful Mary running from me,
Mary standing, not knowing I was watching,
Mary walking forever away.
Mary, always Mary,
across even oceans.

And, always hiding,
with unrevealed ancestral intent,
behind everything Mary did or did not do
in my mind,
in her dainties,
in the very air we swam in,

even now withering in her coffin,
calling always
to her faithful, unfaithful, blessed, cursed,
but always forever,
servant.

Under the Overpass

for Brian

After your little brother died
down by the docks,
I think was the first time
we sat under the overpass.
It was the Saturday night after his wake,
and you told me you had to get out of the house,
away from all the crying.
So we slipped away to my place,
grabbed a six-pack of Dad's beer,
walked down into the trees,
crossed the creek, and up the embankment,
into a darkness darker than the night.
Do you remember what you said?
You didn't say much.
We mostly stared at the creek
and listened to the cars moaning overhead.
And then you said,
"I think the only way I can get over him
is to forget he ever lived."
It made me so sad to hear you say it,
I felt like my guts just fell out of me
and slid down the rocks,
but it was your right to feel that way,

so I just nodded.
I don't know why I'm telling you this.
You know it better than I.

Some Saturday nights,
after the bars closed,
I waited for you under the overpass
and you never showed.
And some nights, I'm sorry,
I never showed,
but some nights we both materialized
out of the dark,
and that's just the way I figured it would always be,
though years might pass between.
The last time I was down there
was the night they said you disappeared,
three nights before they found you
in the grass a hundred yards from your bike,
beside Highway 35.
I think this is what it is
I'm trying to say:
I waited for you all those years,
and you waited for me,
and you waited for your little brother,
all those years,
whether we ever lived or not.

Middle Ground

This fertile earth on which we tread
grows only richer by our blood.
You sink deeper year by year,
my once-dead friends: Will beneath
a fallen tree, Charles beneath
a tractor. Fredrick in the harvester's
teeth. Chris, lying beside
his shotgun in the autumn leaves.
Even Gerald, living still,
in town now, drunk by noon,
pissing himself by four, waits
expectantly for it by the door.
We're told the tall grasses await
the scythe in a firm, deliberate hand,
yet we see only the intelligence
of fire sweep across the land.
We never know the way life was,
only the way it must have been.

The Trees

I used to run, and now I walk,
to the settler cemetery
by the refinery at the edge of town.
I walk back into the trees
where the wilderness is reclaiming
the children's graves.

Why do we always hide them
at the back?
Is it an unspoken shame
we were unable to keep them with us?
Or would it be undignified
to plant them before their elders
in both space and time?
We always cross a distance to find them.

Sometimes I go at night
and stand before the tree line,
and they seem to beckon to me,
but I am too modern for that.
I know the trees end at the creeping
sludge of The Nemadji River
and the flood plain that soaked up
the famous benzene spill,
and beyond that seagulls fighting over garbage,
and I turn gratefully away from the children
to the streets their parents made.

Afterlives

Mary's back beside her parents,
who never wanted her to leave,
between two rows of Lombardy poplars
in the Catholic cemetery.

And maybe her spirit lives on
in God's country,
doing whatever spirits do there . . .
certainly not waiting for me.

Or maybe she's been reborn
at least once already,
maybe as my murderer
or my future mother
or someone I won't meet again
for another thousand lives.

Or is she in the trees
or the clouds already
accumulating above her former life,
beginning now to boil
and drop on us
one atom at a time.

Wherever you are, Mary,
the boys tell me your cat looked for you
for two days after you'd gone,

and then went back
to licking itself in the sunshine.

I don't know what's worse,
the looking for you
or the forgetting.
I don't need to tell you
I always hated that cat.
There, I said it again.

The Human Form

for Merzad

Whether they live or die,
your loved ones will leave you,
your wife and children, your friends
and heroes and leaders will leave you.
You will become an empty house,
inhabited by memories
that one day will leave you as well.

Once I believed in love.
Once I believed there was nothing
more beautiful than Mary.
And then the flames
and then the waves,
and a thousand faces in a thousand scenes.
The world became a canvas for doubt.

The moon becomes nothing but a big rock
that would as soon crush you
as bless the union of lovers.
You sit on the deck after a double shift,
when you should be heading
straight to your bunk,
and you are cursing that cold, senseless rock
when something strange happens.

The indifference of it,

the ease with which it could crush you,
with which it is, in fact, crushing you
this very moment,
startles you with its merciless power,
with its. . . . What is it?
This vaguely familiar thing
you're suddenly feeling?
Is it? It can't be . . .
something like love.

Home for Christmas

That evening grows in my vision
as if it were approaching
rather than receding in the distance behind.

I had been out in the storm all afternoon,
in a dark blue of blowing snow,
building a snow fort to protect us
from creatures emerging
from the murk beyond the streetlight,
until cold and hunger had overcome me
and I went inside.

Mother and Father were in the kitchen,
which glowed like an ember in the dark house,
Mother drawing a pot roast from the oven,
Father working on the dripping faucet.
They were both humming . . .
humming the same song,
she high and he low,
a tune I had never heard before.

I felt suddenly so warm
I thought I might burst into flame
standing there in that kitchen.
Mother turned to me and exclaimed,

"Well now, let's get you out of that getup!"
And Father asked if I'd slain any dragons.
And I stood there, unable to speak,
for fear I'd lose this forever.

I now stare out into another storm
sixty years hence,
and I believe I can see our old home
glowing through the blowing dark,
and I know that day is growing closer
when I will stand before them again,
still alive and still together
and maybe still in love,
and I am so happy
I refuse to deny
I feel flames rising inside.

Folly & Time

for Mary

I recall a great despair
falling over me when I was a child
and my mother left to go shopping,
for everything that happened then
was the first and last time,
and I felt in my bones
she would never come back.
Then I learned the cynical trick
of teenage years,
that nothing was original,
that everything was always repeating,
and we'd always have second chances.
We could take everything for granted.

And I remember us driving home
from your parents, on Christmas Eve of '83.
You were driving because I was drunk,
and you were yelling at me
for swearing in front of your family,
and I called you a bitch,
and you raised your fist in the air between us,
and I caught it in an iron grip
and held it fast,
and in that pose we were frozen,

passing through great dark at great speed,
touching each other for the last time.
I don't know if the children were awake or asleep,
but I know now that everything happens only once.
The next day you asked me to leave,
and that day was forever.

A Fly in Winter

Snow drifts lean in
out of the moonlight,
pressing against the shack from every direction.
Ice squalls tear through the cedars,
stripping them of all moisture,
drawing the scene as close to death as life can get.

I remember standing before the window
of the hunting shack where I had gone alone
when Mary asked me to leave.
I'd built a fire in the Franklin stove and left it open
so firelight shivered on the walls,
and I watched the wind and ice scour the trees,
and the sharp black of space waiting above.

I turned to survey my new home,
a tiny, dying ember in the vast night,
a stripped cot, a stove, an armload of wood I'd dropped on the floor,
a wooden chair, and a table where my gun and bag lay.
I dropped onto the chair and stared
up into the night,
and just like that I was filled with an excruciating delight
at the thought of rising into the darkness.

My hand rises of its own accord and reaches toward the table.
And then, somewhere in the flickering dark of the room,

I hear the thick, drunken buzz of a blue bottle fly.
It strikes me with the substance of a fist,
and I think, how the hell did you survive in here this long?
And my hand falls on a log,
and I feed the fire,
and the fly sustains me on its single note
throughout the night.

Those Years

Us in that tiny apartment together
in that run-down town,
Mary and the two kids always needing and screaming
and me, working after work
after work,
never a moment to just sit and drool,

and the yelling, endless it seemed, the yelling,
so much my hands
would rise sometimes to strike
and I'd fight them back down again, always,
in my mind or in the muscle,
and this afterlife I now call a life
is a heaven for it.

Mary called every Christmas
until her cancer came.
The kids are good people,
better than ever I was,
and sometimes one of them
adds a transfer to a flight
so he can pay me a visit,
show me pictures
of his kids.

I walk along a crumbling street
in a crumbling town

and I feel as worn down
and anonymous as the street itself.
I cross it natural as a plastic bag in a breeze,
and the fighting is a glowing now,
a distant fire warming me
from another life.

Open Swim

Tuesday afternoons I soothe old wounds
in the YMCA hot tub.
I raise my gaze through the steam and see
the children of my youth screaming around me.
Many of them have been dead for over forty years.
I have a hard time of it, remembering some of them,
but here they are, about to die again.
They will go to war so they can go to school,
and they will never come home again,
except in the hot tub visions of old men.
We were made to be broken, beaten, and burned,
but please never take away these days
when we believe we are free.

Mary Sleeping

The sky has gone from red
to black, and everything but the refrigerator
seems to be asleep,
but I lie awake in the stillness
thinking about how things should have been.

Thinking of how I haven't changed,
I remember lying awake like this
when we were all together
under one roof,
Mary asleep beside me still,
with just enough streetlight falling through
the curtains that I could distinguish her profile
from the dark.

And then I would wonder
how I'd ended up there,
through sheer physical labor,
always one step ahead of bankruptcy,
two boys growing headlong toward manhood
in the next room,
a wife growing cold toward me
in the innermost room of herself
and me shipping out again in a day or two.
And I would think about how it

was supposed to have been.
Once I had a dim vision of my future
in which I would go to college,
study biology, and some day make
important discoveries.

I would turn to my side
and watch Mary sleep,
Mary beside me
breathing so calmly
everything seemed alright.

The only discovery I ever seemed to make
was how close a human could get
to lying down forever in the dirt
while staying on his feet.

And now we all lie under different roofs,
and still I play the old game with myself,
wondering where I should be now,
and I suppose where I should be
is where I've always been,
lying here in regret.

Elegy for the Man Everyone Thought I Might Become

No one knew you better than I,
and for that I am sorry.
I held you, wet and trembling,
in my arms,
and made the decision to set you aside,
so I could stand between you
and those who, it seemed, wanted
to fuck you for an extra buck.
I laid you down in your gilded crib
and went to work instead.

Often, in the evening,
I admired the sleekness
of your unweaned beauty,
saw how the world could yearn for you endlessly,
and when morning broke
the news of your latest expectation
I'd put you back in your little casket,
lace up my steel-toed boots,
and kick ass for another day.

Independence

for Merzad

By the time I was ten I knew
every woman in my life had been raped
and every man had been beaten.

I knew a flower is both a flower
and a decoration for a grave . . .
if you can afford it
or not get caught.

I knew freedom is often
as cold and dark
and infinite as space.

And a hand,
until it's held by another hand,
is a weapon.

For Chuck

By this time of night
old men should be asleep,
but here I lie on my cot
in my attic room,
a foot of snow six inches above my head,
looking down into the dark street,
thinking of you, the last romantic I knew.

Remember the vineyard we built
for that guy in the wheelchair
when we were in high school,
and when we visited it twenty years later,
and he was gone
and all the arbors were falling apart,
you took it to heart?

Well, now that you're gone,
I suppose I know how you felt,
but this is what I want to say:
We should never regret the building of a thing
for its inevitable decay.
Promise me that, wherever you are.

The whole house shakes when a train goes by.
It's almost morning. The black is turning blue.
Like every morning for years,
I'll watch the sun rise, a smaller speck every day,
like looking back from beyond Pluto
at all the beautiful bullshit
we leave behind when we go.

Evening

It's evening on the street where no children live.
Flickering light falls from Merzad's window.
He's watching *Lost in Space* reruns again.
Sarah's smoking on her porch, talking fast
to no one in sight. Gary, the registered sex
offender, sits behind drawn blinds,
listening to ABBA on vinyl and crying, according
to Jane, his upstairs neighbor, who watches TV
on mute and listens. And the Johnson kids are cleaning
up the broken glass and guiding their parents
down the dark corridor to sleep again.
Once this world would have weighed on me.
Once I would have wished for another life.
And now? Gary cries and someone listens.

Thaw

The path diverged as I approached town,
and I chose the alley, the army, the struggle,
the chance of death over poverty.

And now, fifty years later,
I have emerged onto the forsaken street,
at a point I may have never reached by other means.

It ends at an empty parking lot
where a fox stands in falling snow,
and nothing else moves
but the bouquets of breath
taken from us by the breeze.

The fox watches me, and I watch it.
Neither of us will move
until one of us moves.

EPILOGUE

Roze & Blud

As the proverb goes,
your best friend died before you were born,
and your true love will be born
after you have died.

And so,
we wander a world between two great loves
that we shall never see,
so let us, at least, be kind to one another
and wish those fortunate few
whose lives overlap to meet,
for the love of us all.